*RAILSPLITTER*

# RAILSPLITTER

REFLECTIONS ON THE ART OF POETRY
COMPOSED IN THE POSTHUMOUS VOICE
OF HONEST ABE LINCOLN, FORMER PRES., US

## MAURICE MANNING

COPPER CANYON PRESS
PORT TOWNSEND, WASHINGTON

Cover art: Steve Cody

Copper Canyon Press is in residence at Fort Worden State Park in Port Townsend, Washington, under the auspices of Centrum. Centrum is a gathering place for artists and creative thinkers from around the world, students of all ages and backgrounds, and audiences seeking extraordinary cultural enrichment.

LIBRARY OF CONGRESS CATALOGING-IN-PUBLICATION DATA
Names: Manning, Maurice, 1966– author.
Title: Railsplitter : reflections on the art of poetry composed in the
    posthumous voice of Honest Abe Lincoln, former Pres., U. / Maurice Manning.
Description: Port Townsend, Washington : Copper Canyon Press, [2019] |
    Includes bibliographical references.
Identifiers: LCCN 2019013621 | ISBN 9781556595714 (pbk. : alk. paper)
Subjects: LCSH: Lincoln, Abraham, 1809-1865—Poetry.
Classification: LCC PS3613.A5654 A6 2019 | DDC 811/.6—dc23
LC record available at https://lccn.loc.gov/2019013621]

9 8 7 6 5 4 3 2 FIRST PRINTING

COPPER CANYON PRESS
Post Office Box 271
Port Townsend, Washington 98368

www.coppercanyonpress.org

# CONTENTS

Every kingdom divided against itself
is brought to desolation, and every city
or house divided against itself will not stand.

Matthew 12:25


Old Abe Lincoln a railsplitter was he,
And that's the way
He'll split the Confederacee.

attributed to Tad Lincoln

ABRAHAM LINCOLN WAS OUR MOST LITERARY PRESIDENT. Indeed, he *made* himself and he found his life's purpose and meaning through reading. It's as if his identity, his sense of self, was composed of the books he read. Lincoln's many letters and speeches often include literary references, demonstrating that his mind was formed not just by present matters or professional duties but more importantly by the broader recognition that meaning and values are handed down to us through the wisdom of those who thought and wrote and acted before us. Lincoln further recognized that citizenship in our country is a solemn task, and that the welfare of our nation depends on *us*. He understood the notion that the government should be a trustworthy representative of the public, and he gave that word capital significance, the *Public*. As the momentous years prior to the Civil War made evident, redefining and returning to our national purpose was unavoidable. In his thought and writings, as well as his embrace of the social contract we hold in common, Lincoln understood the value of revision.

He also had a sense of humor, and a deep love of poetry, music, and theater. That Lincoln loved the arts—even subversive and satiric expression—and understood them to be vital to a healthy society says much about this man's character. That such a generous man came from nothing, from no advantage whatsoever, has been the most moving element of my study. He believed there is something in the world worth reaching for, and so he reached.

And yet, Lincoln was a moderate man. He was not so driven by his views that he excluded the views of others—in fact, he was profoundly tolerant of difference. Lincoln's record on such matters speaks for itself. He applied a steady hand in the face of great tumult.

My own affinities for Lincoln are long-standing. I grew up near his birthplace and I live in the same county where his parents were married. My ancestors were early settlers of Kentucky. All my life I have had a sense of the world Lincoln came from, and meeting him through poetry has seemed, especially in recent years, inevitable. My great-great-grandfather apparently liked to boast that he had voted for Lincoln—twice.

Finally, there was no question in Lincoln's mind as to the cause of the Civil War. In September of 1862, Lincoln presented the Emancipation Proclamation to members of his cabinet. This is how he introduced the document (as recorded by Secretary of State Salmon P. Chase; quoted in *Lincoln: An Illustrated Biography* by Philip B. Kunhardt Jr., Philip B. Kunhardt III, and Peter W. Kunhardt):

> Gentlemen: I have, as you are aware, thought a great deal about the relation of this war to Slavery; and you all remember that, several weeks ago, I read you an Order I had prepared on this subject, which, on account of objections made by some of you, was not issued. Ever since then, my mind has been much occupied with this subject. . . . When the rebel army was at Frederick, I determined, as soon as it should be driven out of Maryland, to issue a Proclamation of Emancipation such as I thought most likely to be useful. I said nothing to anyone; but I made the promise to myself, and . . . to my Maker. The rebel army is now driven out, and I am going to fulfill that promise.

*RAILSPLITTER*

**Gen. Lees invasion of the North, written by himself—**

In eighteen sixty three, with pomp,
  and mighty swell,
Me and Jeff's Confederacy, went
  forth to sack Phil-del,
The Yankees they got arter us, and
  giv us particular hell,
And we skedaddled back again,
  and didn't sack Phil-del.

A. Lincoln, July 19, 1863

## To a Chigger

O itchy beast of tiny figure,
when I scratched myself I made you bigger;
though you began as but a chigger,
  you redder rose,
a pistol-butt without a trigger,
  thus we were foes.

In armpit high or ankle lower
you left me last to be the knower
that you were first to be the goer
  where sweat may trickle,
and I was felled as by a mower
  with scythe and sickle.

Though *felled* hyperbolizes, true,
the minor wounds I got from you,
the itchiness I felt undue,
  a fierce attacking
I never would have dreamed to woo
  from one so lacking.

Yet me you often so infested,
I felt my life had been divested
and bitterness I had ingested,
  in the hotter days
of youth when meaning is contested
  in lofty ways.

But in age and temperament I seasoned
and with your kind I learned and reasoned,
as an older dog contends with fleas and
  resolves the pest
deserves its life, though it has treasoned,
  and takes his rest.

You are a bug of southern climes
yet strangely strode all through my times,
symbolically, a bell whose chimes
   in turn are grating,
refusing love to find that rhymes
   are dull negating.

## Animadversion

I liked to fiddle with the Latin words
  and imagine how they arrived in English.
Awkwardly, because the Mother Tongue
  was dead and her survivors came
as immigrants plucked from the boats of books
  to be re-rendered by Shakespeare,
to overdecorate a suspicious speech,
  persuasion as gold leaf to gild
the convolutions of a mind driven
  by greed or revenge or banality.
The commoner standing in the pit could hear
  how the device tightened the drama,
as the words came flowing from the actor's mouth
  smoother than any flow of Nature,
and therefore sufficient cause to doubt the speech,
  and whatever virtue the actor claimed.
So, language as a means of pure deception,
  and the inadvertent revelation
of the truth in the bare knuckles of the words
  after dramatic circumstance
has whittled down the flowered phrase.
  Romance and reason, piss and gall.
The language accommodates our contradictions,
  our divided selves, and he who claims
never to be divided, whose melancholy
  never makes war with his happiness,
whose malice never cedes to charity,
  will be surprised when the drama turns
the mind against itself, and the metaphor
  approaches but never arrives at justice.
This is true in the churchyard elegy of Gray,
  the mix of elegy and yard,
of the high, unending tone
  and the unknown end,
the unfathomed meaning of a life.

To give the unknown poor the dignity
of time transforms the meaning of Time.
   To say these people in the ground were poets
whose verses are lost is deeply something
   to live with, because it points beyond the reach
of any language, and the mind
   should not be easily turned from such a prospect,
or else the heart objects to pity.

**Upon the Wilmot Proviso**

Very well, I contradict myself
according to the circumstance—
I'll not deny recorded facts
nor seek to justify positions
I didn't take, yet later took.
Conscience has its little Limbo,
the realm where the soul of a thought is stuck,
forever lodged in history.
If one would strive to be in the right,
yet nevertheless be in the wrong,
what then? I know no deist scheme
or transcendental light to lead
the way from such predicament.
Yet to deny the wrong is wrong.
A wrong may be forgiven, but
denial of the wrong implies
there is no wish to be forgiven.
How many men go to their graves
believing they were in the right?
Mythologies are built on this—
actions and consequences and bends
in the truth to cover original sin.
A man who believes he stands above
the law has not sufficiently studied
the law, of either God or man.
This is the sort of proclamation
I'd say to myself when confronting my wrongs,
but even that wasn't enough
to wash blood from my hands or free me
to enter the country of redemption—
if such a place exists at all—
unblemished. Like a long shadow
my compromises have followed me,
to an afterlife far longer than my life.

## A Brief Refutation of the Rumor That I Allowed Willie and Tad to Relieve Themselves in My Up-Turned Hat on a Sunday Morning at the Office while Their Mother Was Attending Religious Services

I will allow a tall hat
can be put to purposes other than
the polite covering of the head.
And the record shows I carried papers
in mine—important papers, too—
and for dramatic effect I'd pull
them out in court, bewildering
my opponents. But that was practical.
The documents intended to prove
my claim were sheltered from the weather
and less likely to be lost.
And having words I'd taken care
to write proximate to the head
from which they sprang permitted me
to ponder them, to keep them, so
to speak, in the nest a little longer,
before they flew into the room
to batter against the smudged windows
of a prairie courthouse, amid
the clangs of the punctuating spittoon.
It was a commonplace to fill
my hat with oats and feed my horse
when I was riding on the circuit.
And the rooming houses where I lodged
had few accommodations, so
the hat was handy as a basin
if a morning ablution were required.
On this occasion, however, the hat
was mere amusement for the boys
who set it on the office floor
and pitched pennies into it,
stepping farther back each round,

as I was reading on the couch.
Their mother was indeed at church.
The weather was profoundly cold
and the privy regrettably distant
from the office, so, boys being boys,
with a famously permissive father,
I agreed to let them use my boot.

## Knob Creek

It watered the farm on three sides—
    gracing the field, my mother said—
        and nearly crossed itself in place
            after place for several miles before

                it emptied into Rolling Fork.
        If you were walking along the creek
    and looked across the way, you could see
exactly where you'd be after

    another mile or two of walking—
        over there would be an hour later,
            were you committed to follow the creek.
                The future wandered through the valley

                winding like a snake in the grass.
                    One day when we were planting pumpkins
                        I looked across the bottom and saw
                    a couple of white men marching

                seven slaves chained together.
            The slaves were singing to pass the time.
        One of the white men was afraid
    to cross a body of water, so all

of the party walked on the western bank,
    and wound along the creek for hours—
        they kept appearing and reappearing
            as they went, upstream, but going south.

        There wasn't a bridge. There wasn't a bridge.
        Gracing the field, my mother said.
    And now I've mentioned old Knob Creek
as if it's gone away. It ain't.

## Three Cheers for the Know-Nothings

When a public man makes a claim designed
to appeal to popular opinion,
subverting the fact that underneath
the claim a more insidious aim
resides, which, when discovered, will prove
to be unpopular, that man
has drawn a line across his throat.
And yet, the public will not have
the truth—which gives the public man
his license and leisure to subvert it.
Our citizens are mean and simple,
expecting hope and hot reaction
at once. If their inclusion in
a scheme or proposition requires
excluding others from the same,
in general, they'll rally to it.
Folly? Selfishness? Or, merely,
the long drag of deprivation,
as an animal dragging an implement
against unyielding ground, when the switch
is smartly applied, continues its way.
And the man who wields the switch is praised—
for the moment, but then he'll be undone.

## Transcendentalism

One of the things the actor's bullet failed
to do was to interrupt the rhythm

of thought, the flow of the mind as it moves around
an encumbrance or wears it down, as water

patiently tames a rock and may, in time,
pass through it freely. Contemplation

is all there is of the afterlife—the mind
continues steadily, not seeking

decision or destination, unable to rest
and yet at ease, because the thought

is always lulling back and forth, as a boat
gently rocking, following the rhythm

of the world. Raindrops dripping off
the eave are keeping eternal time.

The capacity of the mind is oceanic,
it laps and swells and subsides. The sun

flares out of it and then extinguishes
itself in the dark waters of thought,

the divine ditty of the universe,
the endless inner pitter-patter.

## The Sound of the Earth Convulsing

Mother was certain God was coming for us,
and the trumpet of the end of time had sounded,
deafeningly blown by a band of angels.
In the morning, Father went outside to report
the scarecrow had toppled over, an arm
was sticking up and a crow had lighted on it.
It was the winter and the field was barren.
I remember watching a log roll out of the fire
and roll back in again, repeatedly,
until it rested on the coals and blazed
to light as if it had never moved, and then
around daybreak it happened again.
We heard a hillside of shale slide down
the western ridge. By now we were all outside
to watch and Father joked that a shorter ridge
would surely mean a longer day, more time,
and a chance to raise the place a peg or two
closer to real prosperity. But that
condition ever remained a stranger to us.
Three times the bowl of our little valley shook,
and trembled many more, and the sound went around
as if the heavens themselves were crying out.
The last of these convulsions coinciding
with the day to mark my third year living.
The little cabin bounced with the earth, yet stood,
because, as Father said, it was designed
to move—lap joints, pegs, and notches—
not a nail anywhere to make it stiff.
Reckoning now if God himself was the shaker,
I'm not inclined to call it punishment—
I'm not inclined to call it anything,
even if church bells in Boston rang,
suggesting a joy or a grief had come to the land,
for maybe only the earth was shaking itself.

# Little Billy Herndon

### 1. Reading the Law

Why, bless its heart! his mama said,
and smacked the back of Billy's head.

A lawyer-man must stand up tall,
but Honey, you're a tad bit small.

Perhaps another line you'll choose,
or fetch a taller pair of shoes.

I fear you'll wind up with that fool
who never went a year to school.

### 2. Fancy-Dress Ball

There once was a man named Herndon
who fell for a gal that spurned him.
They bowed at the dance,
there endeth romance,
but nevertheless it burned him.

### 3. Writs, Claims, Statutes, Deeds

Like me, ordained by the emptiness of Kentucky,
removed, like me, to the emptiness of the prairie,
and both of us standing before the emptiness,
the physical and metaphysical,
believing surely something is in both,
a cause, a purpose, uneasy steady friendship,
thoughts to keep to ourselves, a world to make,
philosophy, geometry to ponder,
and everywhere poetry to savor,
and even, matchless Billy, a joke to tell.

## Young Men's Lyceum

The piece of poetry of my own which I alluded to,
I was led to write under the following circumstances.

letter to Andrew Johnston, April 18, 1846

Consider a high Hellenic scene in Athens
  and move it to a prairie town
two thousand years later and see what happens.
  Young men trying to improve themselves
before civilization catches up with them.
  It was comedic, an imitation
of intelligence and manner, a parody
  unaware, of various Shakespeare scenes.
No Socrates of the wild frontier to lead us.
  So we led ourselves—imperfectly
at first. Dramatic-recitation shows,
  orations followed by debate,
rightness and eloquence of phrase and pause,
  to sharpen a point with subtlety
then stop, to let it linger in the air.
  What were we seeking? Polish? Praise?
Of course, but we were learning the English language,
  misusing words in order, later,
to use them to greater effect, to clarify
  through metaphor, to make a line
as plumb as the carpenter's bob against the wall
  of reason, in the event that reason
in the world should be discovered to be lacking—
  and we're assembled to raise the barn.
Learning the language deeply shapes the mind
  and there in the lighted mind was freedom
no government could take away and no mob
  could overrule. What we began
in innocence in a dusty tavern room
  was our deliverance from evil.

The journey was poetic, filled with scenes
   whose pathos was both stark and pleasing—
an admirable rhythm was also to be detected,
   as if accompanied by a river.

 CopperCanyonPress.org

# BUSINESS REPLY MAIL
FIRST-CLASS MAIL    PERMIT NO. 43    PORT TOWNSEND WA

POSTAGE WILL BE PAID BY ADDRESSEE

Copper Canyon Press
PO Box 271
Port Townsend, WA  98368-9931

# What do you think?

**OUR MISSION:**

*Poetry is vital to language and living. Copper Canyon Press publishes extraordinary poetry from around the world to engage the imaginations and intellects of readers.*

*Thank you for your thoughts!*

BOOK TITLE: _____

COMMENTS: _____

_____

_____

Can we quote you? ☐ yes ☐ no

☐ Please send me a catalog full of poems and email news on forthcoming titles, readings, and poetry events.

☐ Please send me information on becoming a patron of Copper Canyon Press.

NAME: _____

ADDRESS: _____

CITY: _____ STATE: _____ ZIP: _____

EMAIL: _____

 **Copper Canyon Press**

*A nonprofit publisher dedicated to poetry*

MAIL THIS CARD, SHARE YOUR COMMENTS ON FACEBOOK OR TWITTER,
OR EMAIL POETRY@COPPERCANYONPRESS.ORG

The will of God prevails. No doubt, no doubt—
Yet, in great contests, each side claims to act
In strict accordance with the will of God.
Both may, one must be wrong.
                                    God could have saved
This Union or destroyed it without war
If He so wished. And yet this war began,
And, once begun, goes on, though He could give
Victory, at any time, to either side.
It is unfathomable.


Stephen Vincent Benét, *John Brown's Body*

## By God I Was a Sly Gesticulating Fool

Unfolding myself to rise in court
required a rousing double jerk
that ever proved to startle the clerk,
and the judge, when I rose from a chair too short,
to sail, as a ship listing to port,
and then I'd add flamboyant quirks—
employed that an anecdote might work—
why, I'd tug the whiskers on my wart.

All for emphasis—to make
my homely body homelier,
and let my right hand be a wrench
to the left, to loosen the tale, and take
a mooring sharply at the pier,
unloading reason at the bench.

## John Brown's Baby Has a Cold upon His Chest

If the actor hadn't shot me, I might
have lived, like Whitman and Melville, for most
of my century, the first
president
American born and not from a state

that had ever been a colony—
the new America, settled
ahead of law and reason
by those who believed
sincerely in the promise, whose

design implied the promise, and those
who took it for granted, or took it for
themselves, driven by greed
or necessity,
to move the west much farther west.

Up to the war I can tell you this:
the slave owners wished to extend
a colonial system using
American law
to back it and cover up the sin.

Now if that doesn't sound familiar
then I'm not dead Old Honest Abe.
Getting a law on the books
means future debate
will be confined to the law alone

and exclude the truth, or dare I say,
the moral barb the law is intended
to blunt or cover up,
and so the law
enters the books to serve deceit.

You in later centuries
may like to know how all of this works.
I cannot see your time.
I'm only permitted
to see a few years beyond

my own, and the actor cut it short.
Curious, too, Whitman and Melville
separately described
John Brown
as a meteor, a metaphor

to herald the war, but here the art
is also deceiving, for the skies
of 1859
and '60
were known for meteoric events—

the gleaming, shooting stars were real—
and all the poet had to do
to find the metaphor
was read the news
or lazily look up in the sky.

Another way to think of this
is to imagine poetry
was simply in the air—
as John Brown
would be, suspended by a rope.

And by the way, the actor was there
to see him hang, disguised in the blue
of a US uniform,
to watch the old man drop and kick,

a greater reality, perhaps,
than the actor was used to, the same actor
who with his brother commissioned
the bronze statue
of Shakespeare in Central Park,

for all to see, the Bard himself,
presented by men who played his parts
onstage and were
regaled as men of great refinement.

But I always took refinement lightly,
and that left room for comedy,
a genre, you should know,
the actor thought
was beneath his station and talent, though

after murdering me in the second act
of one he leapt to the stage and broke
his leg, a play within
the play, which produced,
in my final moment of hearing, laughter.

The great tragedian reduced
to play a rude mechanical,
who blunders his Latin line,
hopping across
the interrupted stage to exit.

But the war invited comedy—
why, ladies and gentlemen would picnic
on a hill above a battle
to watch the slaughter,
and dab their mouths with handkerchiefs.

It also welcomed song, at first
austere—the strident "Battle Hymn,"
whose truth goes marching on,
so soon becoming,
John Brown's body lies

a-moldering in the grave, and later,
the farcical, John Brown's baby
has a cold upon his chest.
The melody
was easily adaptable.

And the busy photographers lugging
their boxes of glass plates to the field,
sometimes posing the dead
in genuine bathos,
to show the public what they were missing—

young men, poetically arranged,
who moments before had been singing, reciting
light verse or prayers
under their breath,
when the shadow of death directed the art

of dying should commence at once,
and only the dead were unified.

## Learning to Write with a Feather

The claim my cousin offered after I died,
that he'd killed a buzzard for a single feather
in order to bend my fingers around the quill
that I might learn the shapes of letters, is true.
How strange that I could read most anything
and grasp it. If I read it twice aloud
I could recall it ever after, word for word.
There's a divinity that shapes our ends,
a line from *Hamlet* I used to savor, because
it sounds just right, yet the meaning bounds away
as the mind, desiring comprehension, advances.
And all of this before I could write my name,
for what was printed differed from what was written.
It didn't occur to me in early years
that reading was the offspring of writing,
so getting ahead in reading was backing up.
Though once I began with letters I hadn't ink
or money for it, or paper, and furthermore,
I hadn't anything of my own to say.
So I copied all of *Hamlet* in the air,
from his father's ghost and on to Yorick's skull,
the black feather twittering like a wren.
A single feather representing the bird
in full—synecdoche, I think it is.
My mother, who could read but couldn't write,
presented all of her person with an X.

## On Having a Fondness for Sentimental Songs and Verses

I like the one about the banjo player
who takes his banjo with him when
he meets his friends up in the sky. The verse
says: *some thing else am mighty true,*
*de banjo gwine to be dar too.* The wit
delivered by the primitive voice.
And I can't argue with the theology—
at least it's interesting. If banjos
are allowed in heaven then there's something to do
besides patiently counting down
eternity or basking in holy light.
Not that it matters much to me
in my state of being merely a mind that's tuned,
I suppose, to resonate. Let's call it
a twang in there, a very American twang,
originating from a gourd
and a stick and a few strings. A nonsense song
may have a deeper meaning or not,
or maybe it acquires meaning through time.
That's very American, too—meaning
catching up with time, or time simply
ceasing to matter, and the truth
is left as plain and silent as a banjo
hanging from a peg on the wall.
I like that image, a plain American image,
and some thing else am mighty true—
a banjo with a metaphorical shadow
ironically attached to it.
An image like that, suspended in time, will change.

## The Human Imagination, 1855

Conceiving a mind in torment, as Poe
was known to do, or a heart forever
in grief, in which he also dabbled,
must have a purpose beyond amusement.
Being mad or lonely is too easy,
and neither tries the imagination.
I believe in the value of whim and wonder.
I believe that walking toward the horizon
to become a speck in the distance, one
may not be thinking of anything.
Maybe the body wants to go
and the mind is content to be empty,
or to believe there's nothing in it.
Arriving out of view and alone,
however, the mind is filled like a cup.
Wonders and beauties are pouring out,
an inexplicable passion
has risen like a daisy, and one
may sing or be completely silent
and feel the opposite of alone,
and be at peace and continue on
and leave no record of having been
a person at all, to be seen walking
in the distance, going out of view.

## A Barrel Full of Pickled Pigs' Feet

I received a letter from the son
of a horse doctor in Perryville
who said his father was shot right through
the pocket watch he drew on the page
of his letter, pointing out the hands
were missing now and the face of time
had a 50-caliber hole in it.
The horse doctor was a Negro,
born in freedom, ironically,
who lived in a village of free blacks
the Union had presently burned
to prevent the enemy from shelter.
They were also shooting the horses so
the enemy could not escape.
The horse doctor had a horse
named Jupiter, or Jupe, for short,
who survived and now the boy had ridden
the horse to be taken in by the Shakers,
and he reckoned he would doctor horses
for them and their mules and oxen, too,
for creatures don't know enemies.
An American habit is to fail
to recognize the symbolism
of what happens, even as
what happens always is also real.
The description of the scene the boy
presented in his letter brought
to mind a memory of looking
into a barrel as a boy
myself when I accompanied
my father to the mercantiler
wherever we were living then.
Hundreds of pigs' feet floated
in the brine, and a skim of muck covered
the surface like a cataract

clouding an ancient eye. The hole
in the watch reminded me of the eye,
I guess, because I imagined the boy
living to be an old man
occasionally looking through
the watch to see his father there,
because I liked to imagine things
that touched my heart and gave me hope.

## That Part of the Country Is, within Itself, as Unpoetical as Any Spot of the Earth

That is a claim I would revise
if I were living now. I aspired
to poetry back then. To be
thought of as wise and full of feeling,

to capture something in the world,
to put some words in rhythms and rhyme
and follow the fashion of the time.
A poem had to be sincere,

and it had to be pretty, and the poem
had to reveal the poet's virtues.
Nothing to ruffle the feathers of taste
or to confess a human flaw.

Art and perfection were bound together.
But I won't subscribe to perfect art,
not now. I believe that poetry
is made from absence, out of nothing,

or no place real; the poem flies
as coldly as a hawk, or else
as sweetly as a wren, or it trots
along as an old, blind horse.

The mind is an empty theater
and there is nothing on the stage,
yet from the dark void a voice
begins to sound itself and say

its terrible lines—and then to change them,
to make them smoother, to make them more
than words and more than a dream in the mind.
And then the words in the mind are free,

and the poet, too, is free, until
another voice speaks from the darkness.
I was born and raised in Purgatory,
and I heard many voices there,

one was even my mother's, singing.
Others I heard in books or silence.
And then one day I heard my own,
a voice so clear it startled me.

## The Smell of Open Ground in Spring

My brother's grave unmarked, my mother's too,
and later my sister's, and, finally, my father's.
All of them namelessly entered the ground.
A human history, the sign that's known
because it's missing, how innumerable
existences have come and gone and gone
to dust, and the eye of time refuses to blink.
Someone digging a hole and singing and crying,
then someone loved is dropped in the ground and buried.
No wonder believing in the afterlife
and walking down a street of gold appeals.
What is the point of being alive in the world?
What is the point of watching your mother die?
Or the point of going to her bedside
knowing the knowledge of death had set like the sun
in her mind, and she whispered, Be a good son.
When metaphor and truth become the same,
when the distance is erased between the fact
and the figure representing it, one seeks,
blindly perhaps, another metaphor.
Behind a horse and a plow I opened the ground
in three states, sometimes reading a book
as I went. Once in the middle of *Pilgrim's Progress*
I realized the furrows in the field
could just as well be verses on the page,
and the point of being alive fell down on me,
and the smell of open ground brought me to tears.
While irony may wrap itself around
a poem, the true poem in the end
escapes the shroud. It's the art of resurrection.

## The Long and Short of the Matter

What prompts a long and skinny man
to hanker for a stout woman,
indeed, a woman whose stoutness stands
in marked contrast to the man's
gangly, elongated frame?

The history of human pairing,
my own uncertain tries and erring,
and even after marriage, staring
into the well of wonder, despairing
that such condition wants a name.

Yet humming rhymes delightedly
I found there is a history
conveyed by earthy poetry—
the Jack Sprat Philosophy—
so I denominated the game

as if tranced and danced round in my mind,
recalling Wyatt's hunt of the hind
and Herrick's puns for how he finds
those tremblings of different kinds—
so for my love I found the same.

I died in service of the state,
but the tireless cause did not abate
an instinct I felt to procreate,
or merely heatedly, to mate

      with Mary, short and stout,
      and close the daylight out.

And blindly many times to her I came.

## To the People of Sangamo County

Youth is, for anyone, full of regret
and things to look back on later with more
regret and embarrassment. The effort to be
accomplished, without experience,
is something to pity, and yet to have a life
for which the occupant is also
the designer and guide is greatly to be desired.
For my father, life happened to him.
He lived without imagination, never
believing anything beyond
the facts of present circumstances, which
is a blunt approach to being alive.
His method was an embarrassment to me.
But I couldn't make my way of being
or becoming—as it always seemed—without
demeaning his. How foolish that was,
and simple—that is a greater embarrassment,
a failure of my imagination.
One of the things I've pondered in this gloom
is art, and I've decided the art
I sought and savored most when I was alive,
implied that sympathy is released
by the beauty of the painting or the poem,
or the mirth of the song—even the strain
of a bow drawing across a fiddle string
has something shining out of it
when properly done or when the passion to make
it shine is sincere. There is a light,
and the light passes to another heart.
In my first political speech I proposed,
in terms I thought were eloquent, improving
the river in my neighborhood
and claimed through art its course could be made straighter
and shorter, to benefit the people.
I'd said the river could be improved by art.

But artifice is what I meant—
believing then that nature could be bettered,
not knowing what I was talking about.

## The Gift of Prophecy

Being shot on Good Friday was, of course,
  symbolic, and nicely fit the drama,
and Pentecost coming a few weeks later,
  as I recall, was an unintended
though moving feature of how my tragic death
  would be interpreted in time.
The actor had no idea what he had done,
  but he transformed me and made me a saint,
in the simple terms of American reflection.
  I'm not a saint—and true reflection,
I've learned in the afterlife, requires a longer
  perspective, a lesson Americans
may have to learn again and again and again.
  I was the sixteenth president,
born in dark, primitive emptiness,
  an unimaginable place
that yet must be imagined if what I mean
  symbolically should have a meaning.
What prophecy could come from such beginning?
  I started out from where I started—
if I could see ahead it wasn't far.
  I wasn't a prophet. I was a man.
Always surrounding me was poetry,
  the tales, adventures in the land,
and desire falling short of true desire,
  and words flung out for sound and music
alone, falling down, a shallow art
  and young, in keeping with our nature.
What future lies ahead? A fine question,
  one to consider quietly,
for now I think I've stumbled onto something
  that begs a little pause for a cause.
Nope, not a saint. I am an allegory,
  and that is why I'm still alive.

## The Winter of My Discontent

That was 1862,
and February was the depth,
and yet the grief went deeper still,
continuing as an endless valley,
and I was walking down it alone.
Death was everywhere a fog
over the land, and in my house,
I concluded, was where the fog began.
I was alone, as I am now,
to pronounce my soliloquies in the dark,
and my thoughts did dive down.
Am I a living ghost? What fate
is now foreshadowed by this moment?
How desperate must I be in this scene?
What resolution must I make?
To call for a horse? Where would I go?
Something happens to time in despair.
It ceases to divide, and yet
division was my residence.
So practicing soliloquies
revealed my mind, and the absence of time
gave me, strangely, time to practice.
And I had a discerning audience,
one who was familiar with my voice.

## Honest Abe's Couplet Machine

I wrote to a minister once, and twice misspelled
a very curious word—*sacrifice*—

not knowing at the time the cloud that word
would fill a few years later, a cloud over

a nation whose understanding of the word
I've come to question. Having had my brains

blown out at a theater as a comedy
was playing on the stage has given me,

shall we say, a unique perspective on the matter.
My death was not a sacrifice, but simply

the period at the end of a long sentence,
a sentence too few of my countrymen have read.

And I wasn't the author of it, but the sentence
included me—I was a phrase in the grammar.

As for stumbling twice on *sacrifice*,
it was the middle syllable that stumped me.

## You Sockdologizing Old Man-Trap

I was laughing hard when the bullet entered my mind,
an abrupt idea lodging there unfinished,
and I had brayed like a donkey earlier
in the play. Following such misery
and discord, it was a pleasure to hear laughter,
to hear the uproar of the audience,
and feel my hand involuntarily
reach out and clap my knee, as if it now
again belonged to me. Tragedy
divides and turns on willful, moral division.
But comedy unifies by accident
and the restoration of order is a surprise.
And so by accident I was united,
for a moment, for a little span of time.

## An Old Track in the Woods

When my melancholy was most profound
in younger days, I was tempted sometimes
to follow an old track in the woods
and cease to be, to disappear.
I could wander into oblivion,
to live and die in the wilderness,
as I was accustomed in my youth—
civilization was not my haunt.
Mortality meant nothing to me
when darker feelings were overwhelming.
Why I succumbed to such feelings,
or nearly so, is a mystery,
and remains mysterious after all
these years. I've contemplated it
and can offer few conclusions. There's darkness
in the world, our common experience—
we contend with it, and we ignore it.
And that was my experience.
You can wander off alone and die
or you can fight that loneliness
to do something true for once with your life,
or something in life can call you to it,
like making a country survive itself,
and leading your people through certain darkness,
and leading them even after that.
I did what I could and doubted it,
I saw the track yet turned away.
I looked at the wilderness in the woods
and went on going for a town,
to reach another human mind.
The ambiguity of life
and being alive, that is the mystery,
and there's a common rhythm to it, a joy.
And joy, or my perception of it, saved me.

Irish I was on Dixie  24

## On Silence

Poetry is the art of silence,
the art of knowing when to stop
a word or phrase and let it hang
like a sheet billowing on the line.
And the sudden or unexpected silence
goes hand in hand with what is said
in words or the flowery, natural phrase.
Beginning with the idiom
and moving to the metaphor,
while following the stark rhythms
of thought as they proceed and follow,
is elegance, a wave of the hand
for dancers to come forth and dance
and give the scene a fluid movement.
I see it all in a grand entrance,
meaning I see it as entrancing,
rapt and enthralling all there is.
But what, in fact or dainty figure,
is the scene? People in dark and bright
attire coming closely together
for a dance, for a spinning, exultant reel?
I made myself present for such
events, yet also removed myself,
to step away to pause and reflect.
And stepping away I learned my candor,
I learned how to pass my time in a phrase,
in a measured phrase of poetry,
and that is where I've tried to live.

## Hen Bit

Not lilacs—I recall in spring
flowers spreading over the pastures,
common wildflowers too small
to pick, probably unnoticed
most of the time, although abundant.
Ashy purple leaves shading
the little pink blossoms, and thus
dimming and dulling their hue. Sometimes
the fields from a distance seemed soaked with blood,
a wound for the country always returning,
real and symbolic at once. Like art,
like all Creation, like love, with lib-
erty and irony for all.

## Vulgarity: An Ode

I told the biggest, toughest boy
from Clary's Grove, If you don't hush,
I'll pick you up and spit in your ass.
The coarsest thing I ever said
to anyone. His eyes widened
at the prospect of my boast. And a boast
it was, a saying I'd merely heard,
so not original to me.
But I liked it because it conjured an image
I had to struggle to see, and then
when I saw it clearly, it made me laugh.
And I sought occasions to say the saying
when I was younger, like a riddle
or a dirty rhyme—I liked to hear it.
I thought of it as a jocular
interruption of the air,
because too much solemnity
is duller than a butter knife.
Humble people like to laugh,
but those incapable of laughter
struck me as being already dead
or not sufficiently alive.
And that was the purpose of my life—
to make others feel more alive,
either by wisdom or vulgar phrases
or nonsense, whose sudden utterance
is like the bell of beauty ringing.

## Rhyme Royal on Eloquence

Many eloquent men fail utterly,
which ought to suggest mere eloquence alone
won't do, and, in fact, invites disdainfully
suspicion for the language used by one
who utters pretty polish. The thought is gone
completely, or it's buried beneath a mound
of words, and digging through them, won't be found.

Bad poetry exaggerates
itself, and isn't even practical,
like hitching up a mule to extricate
a rotten tooth. The claim to be radical
in expression doesn't mean original,
just as hanging curtains on the wall
won't make a window for anyone at all.

Nor will the use of figures—metaphors,
antithesis—unbind a deeper meaning
unless the figure clarifies. The door
of insight is flung by composition gleaning
what wasn't known and finding the key. As greening
in spring enlivens the world, transforming it,
so eloquence needs nothing adorning it.

It comes from a voice that has long endured the spell,
the inebriating spell of rhythmic words,
of language reaching beyond what it needs to tell.
The voice has listened to itself and heard
the chaff and chatter, and with itself conferred
and concluded the matter, that eloquence is mainly
confining what is said to say it plainly.

## A Plank from the Platform

Interesting to use the metaphor
of carpentry, as if designing a country
is merely building a stage for the artistry,
by some rough magic, freely to occur.

Some metaphors, like me, are dead, what's more
to have one handy to sling is sophistry,
a little twig, but broken from the tree,
as useful as a patch of briars and burs.

But falling short of the figure is perfect failure,
and I learned more from failing than I learned
from occasions when the words fell into place.

And finding a rhyme for failure? No tailor
could stitch one neatly in the sleeve. They're earned,
the rhymes I mean, like wrinkles in a face.

**Euclid**

Geometry and poetry
have much in common—both
through lines and circular motion define

empty, imaginary space
by giving it a form,
and when the form is beautiful

the logic of design presents
itself plainly, to prove
beauty is never an accident.

Geometry measures the abstract earth,
poetry measures abstraction
in general, to make something

beautiful and true from nothing.
I read *The Elements* through
and found it wanting nothing, meaning

his method could not account for nothing—
irrational numbers skipped
into the cold infinity

a mind like his could not imagine.
But mine imagined it,
and I let it become my metaphor,

my number that refuses to end,
approaching almost nothing
and everything in all directions

at once—my little metaphor
I've carried with me like
a butterfly chained to a chain.

He cannot sleep upon his hillside now.
He is among us:—as in times before!
And we who toss and lie awake for long
Breathe deep, and start, to see him pass the door.

His head is bowed. He thinks on men and kings.
Yea, when the sick world cries, how can he sleep?
Too many peasants fight, they know not why,
Too many homesteads in black terror weep.

Vachel Lindsay, "Abraham Lincoln Walks at Midnight"

## The Fool

Abraham Lincoln is my name
And with my pen I wrote the same
I wrote in both hast and speed
and left it here for fools to read.

Locofocos, Hunkers, Copperheads,
on down to the proud party of Know-Nothings.
*Reductio ad absurdum*—to wit, to wit!
Oh, the names some men willingly give themselves
and wave before them as a sacred banner.
Rightly out of Bedlam came Poor Tom,
a fool's fool, who led Lear back to himself
and spoke the broken language of gibberish.
So I sometimes had to play the fool,
comparing Negroes outlandishly to hogs,
to imply the average hog was treated better.
That was a gross means of understatement,
but understating the obvious allows
the ox nimbly to squeeze through the keyhole.
Although there's nothing nimble about an ox,
getting one through a keyhole makes a mark.
When I needed to be a fool, I applied myself
to the task, feigning a belch when necessary.
And I studied the lines of fools to practice my part,
drolly to bend the language and make it an art.

## The Philosophy of Composition

The *locale* being thus determined,
I had now to introduce the bird—
and the thought of introducing him
through the window, was inevitable.—

That's unintended poetry
from Poe, one of my favorites.
He also said a work of art
should begin at the end, a luxury
I might have enjoyed should I have lived.
I ended not at the end, but the middle.
Poetry relieved my mind
and deepened it, and lifted my heart,
because the language remained alive.
Poe was confident of his talent
and sometimes apologized for it,
whether sincerely I can't say.
It doesn't really matter now.
My verse was coarse, which I accepted,
but composition was a love
I had longer than any in my life,
and versification a noble labor.
Precision won't be precise unless
it's practiced, and parody can be
a useful exercise. Before
I read "The Raven," I read instead
a version about a polecat
and a bumpkin named Jeremiah.
You can imagine all that happened.
That was good enough for me; I found
the polecat very affecting.
A mad mind in the poem, mad
from grief, I understood, but lore
and nevermore and poor Lenore

were tighter than a tick's hatband.
I could rhyme, but never like that.

I suppose introducing a chicken
would not have been inevitable,
but that might have been my kind of poem.
In one of the verses I composed
I was happy to use *skedaddled,*
a rarity in poetry,
but it suited the rhythm of the line
and I liked the flock of consonants,
how the word almost swallows itself.
Say it and feel your throat tickle.

They drugged him on Election Day,
whoever they were, they drugged Poe,
a volume of forgotten lore
himself, and then was nevermore.
His parents, by the way, were actors
from Virginia and, sadly, they were poor.

## Speaking to Mary after a Speech

After giving a speech, most often to men,
eventually I'd wander home and Mary
would inquire about my elocution, whether
I'd hit my mark or fallen short, or foundered.
That was a metaphor my Mary liked.
I liked it, too, because it went two ways
at once, either the so-called ship got stuck
on the bar, or the faithful horse went lame.
The meaning is restrained yet multiplied.
In the primitive country where I was raised someone
would say he's nearly foundered if he'd had
too much to eat. A cow, as I recall,
could founder. I foundered myself, or nearly so,
a time or two, and once it involved cabbage.
I could eat the hell out of some cabbage, and then
go at it again if there were any left.
If a pone to sop the likker in the pot
was not at hand, why, I could drink it down
in a gulp and draw a sleeve across my chin.
It's humbling to be at a speaking engagement
and observe how someone speaking passionately
might still not make a lick of sense, and raising
the passion only digs a deeper hole.
And the argument, when overly explained,
or too voluminous, can lose its footing
in the soup of words—to mix a metaphor—
and sound like diarrhea of the mind.
A mind with the trots, a spew of empty thoughts.
Better to shut your big fat trap
and take a gander down to the fishing hole.
Not that it matters anymore to me.
I'm afraid my days at the fishing hole are over,
as are my speaking engagements, and everything.

# Dogwood

Abraham Lincoln
his hand and pen
he will be good but
god knows When

The red stain in the middle of the blossom
has a legend behind it, part of the larger legend
behind the little twisted tree itself—
that the Cross of Christ, intended to be tall
and stout, to make the burden of carrying it
greater, was made from a pair of dogwood beams,
back when dogwoods rivaled oaks and cedars.
But following the Resurrection, the legend
continues, it was decreed from heaven that never
again would this tree be put to such a use.
So the father of all things shrank the tree
forevermore and bent it down in shame,
a living symbol of shame. The legend was famous
on the old frontier where dogwood trees abounded,
and as a boy I had no reason to doubt it.
I was most intrigued by what the legend said
about the Romans, though—they were inventive
in punishment, and made it a ceremony
and filled it with symbols, and the people watched,
as an audience before a spectacle.
When a punishment is artfully designed
by a nation, one must question whether the nation
has lost its mind. When I was president,
the easterners described me as an ape.
To thank them for their kindness I saved the nation,
in my moment, from those who proposed to be despots.
So far, there is no resurrection for me.
The woods is floweredy, my mother would say,
in spring, when dogwoods bloomed, white clouds
below the taller trees. She liked the renewal

of the season, and longed to hear a good preaching,
although she wasn't an educated woman
and used such common words, such as *floweredy,*
and believed a legend she'd heard about a tree.

# Epigrams for Epitaphs

In my country milk fever laid many low;
with trembling my lovely mother was one to go.

## On the Same

Snakeroot dotted the woods in spring by chance,
and then forever my mother died of ignorance.

## Also on the Same

Who would have thought such a trifling weed
when the milk-cow ate it could do such a deed?

## &c.

There is no syntax for ignominious death,
a rhyme impossible, a waste of breath.

## &c.

The rumor she was illegitimate persisted
and followed me beyond belief, so I dismissed it.

## &c.

O unknown woman in the ground,
for very little you went down.
O irony below the clover,
your life meant more when it was over.

## Testament

I left my father's shadow to build
a boat for a gassy, windy man—
some claimed a brain-rattling man—
whose name was Denton Offutt. The boat
and the enterprise of building it,
and the symbols that presented themselves,
reminded me of Noah's ark,
and I was Noah. Though not rain
but deep snows had melted to flood
the country. There wasn't anywhere
to walk in 1831,
so, ironically, before I built
the boat, I had to reach the place
where I'd agreed to build it, which meant
the manner of my first entrance into
Sangamon County was by canoe.
It was in connection with this boat
that occurred the ludicrous incident
of sewing up the hogs' eyes.
And I decided to include
this tale in my autobiography
when I was running for president,
almost thirty years later.
The people in the East needed
to know what kind of man I was.
If they wanted to vote for the sort of man
who would assist in sewing up
the eyes of thirty hogs, and then
remove the stitching, because a hog
will not go anywhere when blind,
I reasoned I was their candidate.
I took the hogs to New Orleans
and sold them. And took apart the boat.
And sold the lumber by the piece.

And walked back to Illinois,
where I decided to begin
my life in great uncertainty,
as if I were composing a verse
and found the empty page inspiring.

## The Art of Poetry

Everything changes—even alone as I am
in this strange eternity, my mind is restless,
and yet I also live with a kind of peace.
To say I also live, even though I'm dead,
is funny—I have to humor myself down here—
or up here, whatever adverb designates
this realm. Let's call it the realm of the voice in the mind,
and as the mind changes, so must the voice.
But the voice eventually ceases to be distinct
and therefore becomes itself. I don't know how
that happens. It just becomes a common voice,
a voice that anyone hearing it would know.
Ideally the voice will say something worth saying,
or better, say something without having to say it.
Poetry speaks about the unspeakable.
It's a clanking wagonload of paradox
pulled by a horse across a vast land
in utter darkness, and the voice, without
a body, guides the horse. Nothing about
this arrangement seems to bother the horse. Pulling
the squeaking wagonload of paradox
through the darkness, with a voice delivering
a grunt or a doubtful line or a metaphor
to continue on, is all the horse has known.
I suppose the horse is older than the voice.
He's been coming from and going to Forever
forever. But the mind behind the voice,
while often at some repose as I have said,
is also restless, thinking the next new thought,
or thinking nothing, to say something about it
in a manner some would deem beautiful.

## Ballad of Pigeon Creek

'Twas summertime on Pigeon Creek,
the fireflies lit the sky,
I was a lonesome rhyming freak,
born to the world to die.

Verses were my buttered bread,
repast of great delight
to fill my empty-bucket head
with rhyme to say and write.

Declaiming, I would find a stump
and stand upon it tall—
the word I think of now is *bump*—
I cannot rhyme them all.

The lasses were fair, the lads were strong
way down on Pigeon Creek,
inheritance was our lowly song—
by God, we were the meek.

Our schooling was a comedy,
but I could pull the thread
cut from the cloth of tragedy
through all the books I read.

And doing that is what I done,
as freely as the breeze,
and barefoot as a simple pun
below the shady trees.

But books were scarce on that old stream,
back in the way-back-when,
and finishing one, as in a dream,
I'd start the book again.

There isn't a chorus to this song,
nor wisdom here to seek.
It ends like the wind blowing along
the banks of Pigeon Creek.

## *Aside.* Wormwood, wormwood

Trippingly on the tongue, so Hamlet says,
How lines must be delivered from the stage,
Especially when passion must be tempered,

And gestures must not be overdone, or else
Chaos will upend the unity desired.
The groundlings, claims this son, are capable
Of nothing but dumb-shows and noise, nicely
Reaching beyond the stage to pander and pun,

Which makes one wonder how serious is this
Entreaty, then, to hold the mirror up to
Nature? In the play within the play, a mouse-
Trap catches a king unnaturally.

*To be, or not to be* was never my pick.
O, *my offense is rank* is the better speech—

Heaven is how high it smells, the offense—
Enlivened language for murder, ironically.
Low act, but elevated thought, to play
Lightly a scene of wretchedness and folly.

He knew that undeceiving fate
Would shame us whom he served unsought;
He knew that he must wince and wait—
The jest of those for whom he fought;
He knew devoutly what he thought
Of us and of our ridicule;
He knew that we must all be taught
Like little children in a school.

Edwin Arlington Robinson, "The Master"

## When One Is with Strong Wind Oppressed

Give me the spark
of Nature's fire,
that's all the learning I desire—
though all the wisdom
learning lends
will never make amends
for difficulties
scatological,
windiness
that's pathological;
though leaders toot,
there's other fruit
posterity
must find—
sagely doodles left
so silently behind,
or a smear of rhyme
in broken time,
maybe to remind
that *constipation*
loosely rhymes
with *nation.*

For the Union
I was knotted,
as t's are crossed
and i's are dotted:
how oft repairing to
a dogged verse
relieves the anguished
human curse,
and certainly
won't make it worse.
So here's a toot

for the USA,
a living burden
to my dying day.

## The End of Days

I haven't really had an end,
only this strange existence
that is like a portion of my life
when I was first alive
and keeping many thoughts to myself,
some of which were frivolous.
A Mississippi River of thought,
including what I must call
oxbow excursions, has flowed
almost stoically through
my mind since my untimely death.
I haven't laughed away
an afternoon in this somber place.
When something funny
crosses the vastness of my mind, it's like
a piece of driftwood,
of little consequence to the river.
But death may dampen humor—
if any merriment occurs
around here I must invent it.
If there be fiddles here to saw
a feller through the night,
I'm plumb perplexed in finding one.
So, there's a small invention—
reminds me of living in Kentucky—
to make up something against
the nothingness around. A pleasure
accompanies the task.
It's a way to pass the time, or a way
to avoid the obvious,
and let's be honest, I did not reach
the Hallelujah Shore.
I'm having to do this all alone,
all of this invention,
which is a way to praise the darkness,
if darkness is what comes after the end.

## The Audience

Who are you people anyway?
Does hearing my voice from the dead disturb you?
You're probably wondering what to make
of this performance. I wonder, too.
But it doesn't matter to me—I'm dead,
as dead as words writ on the page.
You have to find the life in them,
that is the pleasure of listening
to a voice on the stage or reading a book.
There's something alive you bring to life
by being the reader or seeing the show,
and that makes being alive less lonely.
All of this . . . expression . . . has been for you.
I beg your pardon, I had to pause
for a moment to think of the proper word.
I expect you know how difficult
it is to get the words just right.
*Expression* is too precise, it's better
to think of this as a series of notes
and meditations which, by nature,
are incomplete. One of the things
you have to accept in life and art
are the parts left out, the missing pieces,
and the simply inexplicable.
What's missing says something by being absent,
it is a gesture of the mind
to leave it out, and then the gesture
of another mind to grasp the absence.
But once the absence is grasped, it becomes
a complicated emptiness.
To fill it we have the stage and books,
but increasingly I find that musing
on the emptiness is pleasant enough,
as when looking over a landscape one
can see where a tree has been, even

a wilderness, and contemplate
what might have happened and imagine why.
What else do you want from my countenance,
from my exhausted face staring out?

## An Essay on Man

Happiness is our being's end and aim—
that's quoting Pope, who could turn a useful phrase—
but this is the sort of claim I could believe
if not for myself then on behalf of others.
And I endeavored to share this wisdom, now
I realize, because it sounded wise
and the average person could agree with it.
But, strangely, I lived at a time when the human condition
was going up for some but down for others,
and wisdom could not be equally applied.
And neither was happiness the aim of all.
Ever study Jefferson Davis's face?
Tedious, hollow, a deeply unhappy man.
A cultivated mind is what I called
an education, and the metaphor
of farming for thinking was easy to extend—
a small plot when properly worked shall yield.
In innocence I believed the laborer
could receive an education and profit from it,
and one day be more than merely a laborer.
But a cultivated nation administered,
one may assume, by cultivated men
must allow the common laborer to rise
and better his station—if not, then cultivation
of any sort has ceased to be the subject.
That was my prairie lawyer's argument—
practical I suppose, and happiness
was only part of it by implication.
Had I actually composed an essay on man,
according to my experience, it would
have been a satire to a point and then
descending, ending bluntly to show that a mind
uncultivated will never know freedom
and may have no desire for it otherwise.
A man may be a lowly creature, or be made

to be one, or be one by his own design.
I took a turn at being each of these.
But oppression of any lowers us all, I reasoned,
so I stood up one day, above my station.
My aim? To make a principle practical,
and not to doubt that I could do it, but
to wonder whether in the end it would matter,
though still go forward with my aim. My report?
The war I most fought was in my mind—
skirmishes are occasional, yet persist.

## Nonce

A life exempt from public haunt,
decries my present circumstance,
here tapping, in this nothingness,
the prosody of my Address
or second inaugural speech, a dance
of death, though malice not to flaunt,
composed by me, whose face was gaunt.

One wants one's words to resonate
and yet convey with comprehension
the clear appeal of hopefulness,
as rhythm renders lightly less,
if grave despair is in ascension,
and words are sought to designate
what deeds have done to consecrate.

Decorum in my day was sought
by highly born as well as yokel,
an aspiration to think regardless,
though not adorn in fancy dress
sublimity, but to make it local,
revealed by clarity, the thought:
a future by its past is bought.

## A Synonym for Life

Sometimes the details are alarming—
in the middle of 1862
receiving my hero's snuff-box,
for instance, as if it would inspire.
Perhaps it did. I do recall
I sniffed it many times and felt
not quite alone in my position.
I was environed with difficulties
of mind and decision, piteous scenes.
Wagons of amputated arms
and legs—going to graves for limbs
surrendered by men who now would live
with part of themselves already buried.
Destruction plotted and carried out
for preservation and new creation—
an irony as vast as the land
on which the destruction was conducted,
nothing to hold it all together,
no saying or rhetorical claim
other than knowing history,
eventually, will make a chapter,
however brief, of all that passes.
Whether later generations
will care to read the shorter ones
has not been my concern. The country
was founded not to suppress but to lift
the common life. I learned that life
requires connection to the dead.
A synonym for life may not
be death, but the closeness of the two,
one's dependence on the other,
has long absorbed my study, and that
is plainly written on my face.

## Reading Burns as a Boy below a Tree

My body, straight as the hour hand of a clock,
protruded from the trunk, and the spreading tree
itself now creaked, the very spindle of Time.
Wherever I was, at Pigeon Creek, or a tree
stubbornly standing on the old prairie.
As the sun made its arc across the summer sky,
I'd rotate clockwise every hour or so
to stay in the shade, moving through time, as ever,
propping my head against a root, a book
spread open in my hands, my mind alive
to the difficult dialect of the poetry,
but saying it aloud I was nearly singing,
and yet becoming a lower branch of the tree.
A boy reading a book beneath a tree,
a boy becoming part of the book and part
of the tree at once, the scene and symbols tied
so tightly together they cannot be undone.
The weight of death was not upon me yet—
nor was being American yet a weight—
only a son, a farmer's son with a book
in his hands, lolling beneath a giant tree,
saying the verses aloud—the love, the work,
the love the work discovered, the verse the love
composed and set in rhythm to be said—
the little life and the larger life compared,
though bound together, belonging to each other.
The lessons of the young and foolish that haunt
an older mind, so it believes the blessing
from before, the earlier, innocent time of being,
and being alone in work or verse one learns,
though still I cannot frame a toast to Burns.

## I Sends This for You to Look At You Must Not Laugh At It

The man apologizes for his verse
and adds an *a* to never;
his birth began both life and curse,
a doom almost forever.

A man whose education was none,
whose freedom was bound by locks,
but once Emancipation was won
he became Hannibal Cox.

He said, Let every heart be true,
and may God defend the right,
for we have glorious work to do,
the Stripes and the Stars of Light.

And on his verse I've puzzled long,
until my brow is worn:
a slave may better sing the song
than one to freedom born.

So the hopeful letter he sent to me,
that history may tell
the bonds of love in poetry,
and then he said farewell.

The verse I read of this young man
went with me when I died—
the pages trembled in my hand,
and finishing I cried.

## Madstone Alexanders

I was a superstitious son of a biscuit-eater
and couldn't abide robbing Paul to pay off Peter,

so to speak, as a matter of principle—yet personal life
was different, concerning the boys, an extravagant wife.

I was indulgent with them, protective, whatever they needed
I provided, believing happiness, when so well pleaded,

deserved my attention. Their delight gave me delight.
And that was how I loved when alive, and now, in this night,

I grasp the imperfection, but what else should one do?
You love your people and do what love requires of you,

if suddenly love demands of body and mind,
for example, going to the ends of the earth to find

a primitive conjure-woman who owns the only stone
around imbued with healing powers for body and bone.

I did it for my boy who was bitten by a dog
and the stone prevented him from going mad—a fog,

a total fog, recalling now such desperation,
and to think how desperately I also loved the nation.

I was a father of boys, and fathered ideas, too,
and stubbornly, America, I fathered you.

## Belonging to the Ages

I play in a play belonging to the ages
in silences ringing out, as if designed
by a mind whose poetry is empty pages.

The only player, too, on darkened stages,
artistic in my way, though not refined.
I play in a play belonging to the ages.

But theaters are merely painted cages,
rooms to watch imagination confined
by a mind whose poetry is empty pages.

In life I borrowed lines from all the sages
and found myself to airy nothings inclined
to play in a play belonging to the ages.

A tempest in this narrow house still rages
as if the service of the dead is assigned
by a mind whose poetry is empty pages.

A house divided? O formless form, whose wages
must endlessly be paid, yet not divined.
I play in a play belonging to the ages
by a mind whose poetry is empty pages.

## Railsplitter

I was killed by an actor, a famous, glamorous
young man, known for playing the tragic roles.
And I was a president, whose face was coarse

and enigmatic, though marked by a conscious mole.
But the derringer he stuck behind my ear
produced, in the end, a dark, symbolic hole,

American and bottomless. No tears
can fill it. Your Melville had the accurate verse:
What like a bullet can undeceive! Hear, hear—

the antique eloquence of the national curse?
What an ironic martyr I've been. I'm long
in a realm that has no ceilings, though dying was worse.

There is a mystery to being wrong
and that has darkened the shadows of my mind,
mainly, I mean, how I could like the song

"A-way down yonder in the land of cotton"—for rhyme
and, what else should I call it but, jauntiness—
and ignore the euphemistic "old times."

Make up a song to cover sin, boundless
and almost unimaginable sin. My task
has been to stare it in the face, faceless

though it is. We share a common dark. A masque
is what we have—one voice and total silence,
and verse intended not to answer, but ask

the obvious question hanging in the distance
of Time. Who is that swinging on the gallows,
my friends united by love and innocence?

And who is buried in those endless rows,
those silent lines of American poetry
where metaphors and muses refuse to go?

"Gen. Lees invasion of the North, written by himself": Lincoln composed this doggerel with obvious satisfaction. He did not deliver his more famous Gettysburg Address until November 19, 1863. The Battle of Gettysburg raged for three days, July 1–3, 1863.

"To a Chigger": The verse form is the "standard Habbie," made popular by Robert Burns, Lincoln's favorite poet.

"The Sound of the Earth Convulsing": Reference is made to the New Madrid earthquake, which was a series of three major quakes beginning in December of 1811 and concluding on February 12, 1812, Lincoln's third birthday.

"On Having a Fondness for Sentimental Songs and Verses": Reference is made to "Picayune Butler's Come to Town," a song Lincoln requested John Hay sing while visiting the battlefield of Antietam, late September 1862.

"A Barrel Full of Pickled Pigs' Feet": The Battle of Perryville was fought October 4–5, 1862, and ensured Kentucky would remain in the Union. The Shakers, who were pacifists, had a community nearby.

"That Part of the Country Is, within Itself, as Unpoetical as Any Spot of the Earth": The title is a description Lincoln offered in a letter to Andrew Johnston on April 18, 1846, in reference to the region in southern Indiana where Lincoln spent his later youth.

"The Long and Short of the Matter": Lincoln married Mary Todd on November 4, 1842, in Springfield, Illinois.

"To the People of Sangamo County": The spelling of Sangamo County, Illinois, was eventually changed to Sangamon.

"The Winter of My Discontent": The only man executed for his involvement in the transatlantic slave trade, illegal since 1820, was Nathaniel Gordon, a ship captain from Maine. Gordon's ship, the *Erie*, was intercepted by the US Navy on August 8, 1860, with 897 captured Africans aboard, most of them children. The captured Africans were returned to Liberia. Following Lincoln's stay of execution, itself an interesting document, Gordon was hanged on February 21, 1862. Lincoln's beloved son Willie died in the White House on February 20, 1862.

"Honest Abe's Couplet Machine": See Lincoln's letter to Rev. J.M. Sturtevant, September 27, 1856.

"You Sockdologizing Old Man-Trap": From *Our American Cousin,* this line is rumored to have been the last delivered from the stage at Ford's Theatre before Lincoln was shot on the evening of Good Friday, April 14, 1865.

"Rhyme Royal on Eloquence": Reference is made to Lincoln's "Eulogy on Henry Clay," July 6, 1852.

"The Philosophy of Composition": Reference is made to Edgar Allan Poe's essay of the same title, published in 1846.

"Epigrams for Epitaphs": Lincoln's mother, Nancy Hanks Lincoln, died of milk fever, October 5, 1818. Nine-year-old Lincoln helped his father make his mother's coffin. She was buried in a grave that went unmarked until 1878.

"When One Is with Strong Wind Oppressed": The first lines borrow and vary lines from Burns's first "Epistle to John Lapraik."

"I Sends This for You to Look At You Must Not Laugh At It": See the letter and verse sent to Lincoln, March 30, 1864, by Hannibal Cox, 14th US Colored Troops, Co. 8, Chattanooga, Tennessee.

"Madstone Alexanders": A madstone, thought to have medicinal powers, was the colloquial name for a large hairball sometimes found in the stomachs of ruminant creatures.

# ACKNOWLEDGMENTS

My studies of Lincoln and his times have been enriched by the excellent Library of America edition, *Lincoln: Speeches and Writings,* edited by Don E. Fehrenbacher. I also made use of David Herbert Donald's fine biography, *Lincoln,* and of an earlier short biography, *The Life and Writings of Abraham Lincoln,* by Philip Van Doren Stern.

I am grateful to the staff of the national park facilities related to Lincoln's birthplace and early years in Kentucky, Indiana, and Illinois, and to the staff at the Lincoln Presidential Library and Museum in Springfield. I also visited Ford's Theatre and the adjacent museum and was aided by the kind and helpful staff at this important repository. The photograph of the US Capitol before the dome was installed is reproduced with permission from the Library of Congress. The cartoon image of Lincoln playing a banjo is reproduced with permission from the Library Company of Philadelphia.

I would also like to express my appreciation to the editors of the following magazines and journals where some of these poems were first published: *Garden & Gun, The Hampden-Sydney Poetry Review,* and *Plume.* And thanks to everyone at Copper Canyon Press.

*Railsplitter* is Maurice Manning's seventh collection of poetry. His previous books include *One Man's Dark*, *The Gone and the Going Away*, *Bucolics*, and *A Companion for Owls*. His first book, *Lawrence Booth's Book of Visions*, was selected by W.S. Merwin for the Yale Series of Younger Poets. His fourth book, *The Common Man*, was a finalist for the Pulitzer Prize. Manning's poems have appeared in *Five Points, Garden & Gun, Image, The New Yorker, Ploughshares, Plume, Time, The Yale Review,* and elsewhere. A former Guggenheim Fellow, Manning has held a writing fellowship at the Fine Arts Work Center, a residency at the Hawthornden International Retreat for Writers, and an Al Smith Fellowship from the Kentucky Arts Council. Manning is a member of the Fellowship of Southern Writers. He teaches at Transylvania University and in the MFA Program for Writers at Warren Wilson College. Manning has also been a regular faculty member of the Sewanee Writers' Conference. He lives with his family in Kentucky.

Poetry is vital to language and living. Since 1972, Copper Canyon Press has published extraordinary poetry from around the world to engage the imaginations and intellects of readers, writers, booksellers, librarians, teachers, students, and donors.

WE ARE GRATEFUL FOR THE MAJOR SUPPORT PROVIDED BY:

THE PAUL G. ALLEN
FAMILY FOUNDATION

Lannan

TO LEARN MORE ABOUT UNDERWRITING
COPPER CANYON PRESS TITLES,
PLEASE CALL 360-385-4925 EXT. 103

WE ARE GRATEFUL FOR THE MAJOR SUPPORT PROVIDED BY:

Anonymous

Jill Baker and Jeffrey Bishop

Anne and Geoffrey Barker

Donna and Matt Bellew

John Branch

Diana Broze

The Beatrice R. and Joseph A.
Coleman Foundation Inc.

The Currie Family Fund

Laurie and Oskar Eustis

Mimi Gardner Gates

Nancy Gifford

Gull Industries Inc. on behalf of
William True

The Trust of Warren A. Gummow

Carolyn and Robert Hedin

Bruce Kahn

Phil Kovacevich and Eric Wechsler

Lakeside Industries Inc. on behalf
of Jeanne Marie Lee

Maureen Lee and Mark Busto

Peter Lewis

Ellie Mathews and Carl Youngmann
as The North Press

Hank Meijer

Gregg Orr

Petunia Charitable Fund and
adviser Elizabeth Hebert

Gay Phinny

Suzie Rapp and Mark Hamilton

Emily and Dan Raymond

Jill and Bill Ruckelshaus

Cynthia Sears

Kim and Jeff Seely

Richard Swank

Dan Waggoner

Barbara and Charles Wright

Caleb Young as C. Young Creative

The dedicated interns and
faithful volunteers of
Copper Canyon Press

The Chinese character for poetry is made up of two parts:
"word" and "temple." It also serves as pressmark for
Copper Canyon Press.

The poems are set in Sabon.
Book design and composition by Phil Kovacevich.